VOL. 2

# Flower
## Mandalas Patterns

ADULT COLORING BOOK DESIGNS

STRESS RELIEF COLORING BOOK

# COLOR TEST PAGE

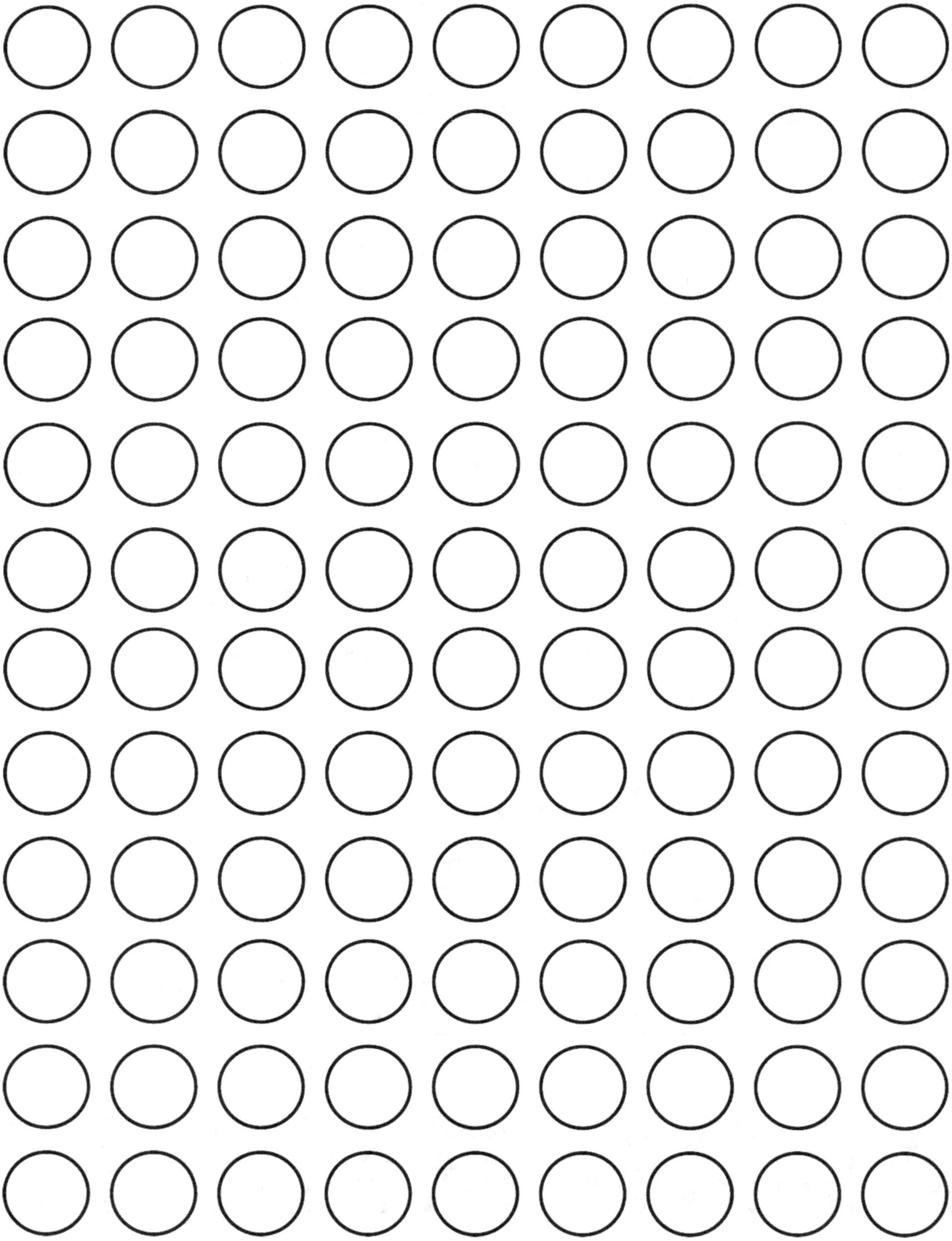

# COLOR TEST PAGE

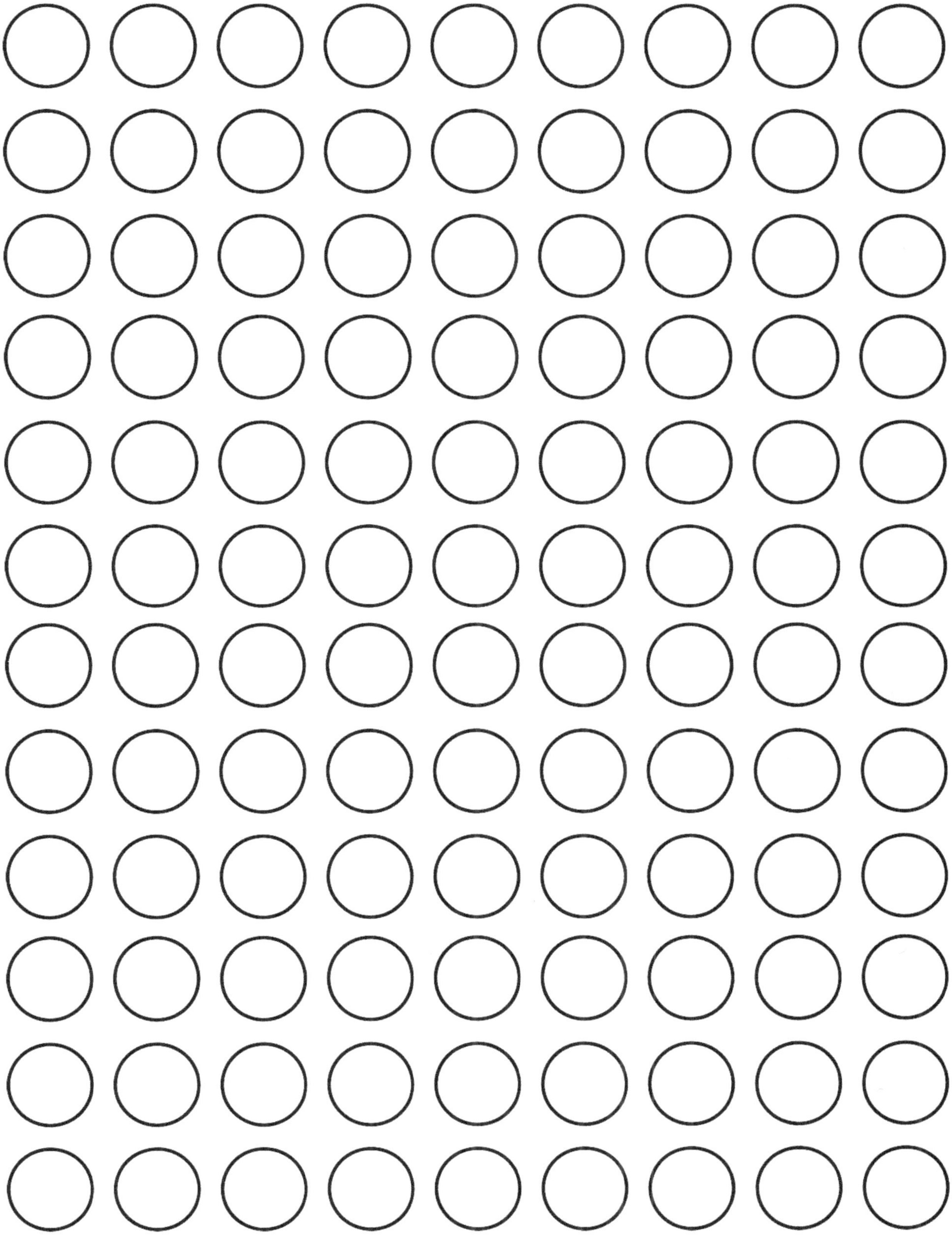

www.ingramcontent.com/pod-product-compliance
Lightning Source LLC
Chambersburg PA
CBHW081751280526
45789CB00008B/2818
* 9 7 8 1 5 3 7 4 3 2 7 5 5 *